It Is What It Is
By
Leah Maye

Copyright © 2024 by Leah Maye

All rights reserved. No part of this book may be reproduced or used in any manner without written permission of the copyright owner except for the use of quotations in a book review.

All Night

I've been awake most of the night
Slept two hours
It's not on purpose
I just can't sleep
I got the text you sent
Still trying to figure out what it meant
I wish you would text in words instead of song
So easily misinterpreted
The lyrics can mean different things to different people
and different situations
Why that song
And why tonight

Conflicted

Consumed with the memory
Consumed with what could have been
Consumed with what was
Emotions are conflicted with the things you say and the things you don't say
The things you do, and the things you don't do

It's not like I was planning our wedding.
But when you said you're never getting married again,
It hurt to know that you never had faith in us.

Too Much

You say you're too much
That I'll hate you one day for just being you
It's you that I love
And you love me
It must be
It isn't too much
It's just the right touch
We go back and forth because life is trying to keep us apart
But that's only because they're jealous of the love in our hearts
For each other
Forever

Ping Pong

It's a game I used to be good at, until we replaced the ball with my heart
This organ can't take the beating of the back and forth
This heart can't take the losing of something that was once sacred

Kiss

Kiss upon a star
My bleeding heart is breaking.
My love is decreasing
One kiss ignites it
One day without you kills it.
Round and round we go.
Will we make it
I don't know

I wish I could go back in time and fall in love with you when it was the right time for us both.

Pissed Off

I'm so pissed off and you know why
I'm not shy about letting you know
Any of my feelings
If you have to ask me then you
Don't even know me
And at that point, why keep trying?

Neon Light

Sometimes we see the signs but
Ignore them no matter how red the flags
We are given signs
The one you just had was a big, bright, neon light
Flashing
Danger, danger
You must break free
I fear if you don't,
It will kill you
I will miss you

Bedtime

A place of darkness, but a peaceful one
The desire to sleep, yet a desire not to miss out on everything
It's hard to keep the balance
It's hard to keep going
It's hard to give up

It sucks that I love you more than you love me.

No

It's not a bad word
Can I touch touch you?
No
Can I degrade you?
No
Can my 13 year old self go to a concert in a tough, unknown city with friends you've never met?
No
Can I touch a hot stove?
No
Do you want to be my plus one to this thing?
No
Do you want to be mine?
No
We have choices
How others react to our choices...
That's their choice
Choose wisely, but don't be afraid to say
No

Pro Choice

We are told to be responsible
But what do we do when our methods fail
Save yourself for marriage, though I bet the majority of you haven't
Even married people make mistakes
But using birth control is against some religions
So we go on to make babies we don't want or can't take care of
What if that baby has a genetic disease or disability
We're supposed to love everyone
But some of us know we don't have the patience, the ability, the confidence, the resources,
You can tell me what to do with my body
Can I tell you what to do with yours
Hypocrite

Bloody

This is going to be a mess
It won't be easy for anyone
I fear the bloody battle
But I also welcome it with open arms
It just needs to end the way it's supposed to
End

You will continue to purposely push me away while I continue to get hurt by you.

Then I Bleed

I'm dry so I drink
I'm empty so I eat
I cut then I bleed
I'm tired so I sleep
I'm awake so I think
I cut then I bleed
I'm anxious so I pace
I'm depressed so I cry
I cut then I bleed
And then I bleed
And I bleed
I bleed

You Ran

You told me to run
I told you to shut up
You told me to run
I told you to stop pushing me away
You told me to run
But I wouldn't
I couldn't
I didn't
So you ran instead
I never wanted to call you a coward
But you were scared and you ran
Do you expect me to call that brave?

Paranoia

Things turned upside down
Stuff gone missing
The toilet seat is always up
There's a thunderstorm in my closet
There's a ghost across the street
Objects turned sideways
What goes up, never comes down
Sleep resets the cycle

I had your back. Why didn't you have mine?

Some Days

Some days I sleep too much
Some days I don't sleep at all
Some days I miss you
Some days I don't
Some days are like hell on earth
Some days are like heaven
Some days I miss you
Some days I don't

Games We Played

You're getting warmer, you're getting colder
Red light, green light
Simon Says
Mother May I
Sure, they were fun
But we didn't gain anything about real life
Real life has to be played massively different
Some of us win
Some of us lose
Some of us cheat
Unfortunately we all have to play
Race against time to win
Race against haters who want us to fail
Race against ourselves to be the best of the best
Sometimes the best you can do is survive

Knew Me

I never knew myself
Until you came along
I suddenly had an identity
A self that was hiding from everyone else
I never knew what I was capable of
And what I wasn't
Until you came along
Then I suddenly knew myself
I know me
But you never had that chance to meet her

Missing you and your tiny shoes. Baby giggles and calling you Bugaboo.

Make Me Yours

I don't want compliments on my smile
Or my eyes
I don't want to be told I'm pretty
How do you make me yours?
Look at me like you've never looked at another
Look at me like I'm the only one there
Hold my hand
Play with my hair
Tell me you love me
And mean it

Words and Actions

You can say it all you want, but you know you won't do it
You know you have to
Get off your ass and make it happen
Only you can do it
Only you can sit around and do nothing
Words mean nothing without actions

Wake up. Smile. Kick ass. Do it again. Do it until there aren't any asses left to kick. And then once more for good measure.

The Fault in Me

I love too hard
I give in too easily
I forgive too quickly
I trust too easily

They Say

They say absence makes the heart grow fonder
They say you always hurt the one you love
They say love hurts, love stinks, love will bring us together
Enough with the metaphors
The truth is
Love does not exist

Last Night

Last night I heard my neighbors having sex
Mostly her
Why do some people sound like they're in so much pain, when it should feel good?
Why do I feel slightly jealous?
Why do I feel slightly turned on?

Stop apologizing for everything. Stop doing things you have to apologize for.

Could Have Had

You could have had me and
I could have had you
But there were problems we just
Couldn't fix
Your fear and my jealousy
I could have had you and
You could have had me

Hostage

You stole my heart and held it hostage
We never dated or had a relationship
But I miss you more each day
I can't let go
My fingers bleed
How can I release the love of someone who never gave me a chance to stop loving them

Repeat

I don't love you
I never did
Repeat, repeat, repeat
I'll find someone perfect
I'll find someone better than you in every way
Repeat, repeat, repeat
Your disrespect to me
Made me disrespect myself
Repeat, repeat, repeat
I think only positive things
I will be okay
Repeat, repeat, repeat
I think only positive things
I will be okay
I think only positive things
I will be okay
Repeat, repeat, repeat
Repeat, repeat, repeat

If knowledge is power, why are there so many stupid people in positions of power?

Our Hearts

Our hearts have been friends a long time
Even before we knew it
Our hearts are infinitely intertwined
Even when I don't want them to be
Our hearts belong together
Even though it seems an impossibility
Our hearts will yearn for each other in death
Even though we will never be

Fickle

Make up your mind
If you want me then be with me
If you don't want me then don't be with me
Don't push me away one day and try to love me the next
Don't break it off with me then change your mind a day later
Don't treat me like no one
Then treat me like your true love the next day
Make up your mind
Before I make it for you

Elusive

On a daily basis
I struggle to find
The elusive darkness they call
Sleep
Sometimes, I catch it
Other times, it never shows
Bastard Sandman

I've thought about giving up. But if I did,
Who would do the
Fighting?

Sin

Carry me to the dark side
Control me with sin
The devil himself
Can't help but grin
Put your mark on me
Burn my skin
Complete trust and loyalty
Cover me with sin

Bye

I won't hold on to the thread anymore
It's too thin
It frays and stretches then
Finally snaps

You keep letting me down. The worst part is, I keep letting you let me down.

Familiarity

Wake up
Go to work
Come home
Go to bed
Do it again
And again and again
There's comfort in the familiarity
There is peace and happiness
There's hopelessness in the familiarity
There is regret and missed opportunities
The mundane isn't all bad
A mundane lifestyle is a drama free life

Yesterday

Yesterday seems so far away
Tomorrow seems so close
Yesterday wasn't so long ago after all
Tomorrow is coming quickly
All I want is yesterday back

Water

I need a taste of you
Just one drop
You're a tall glass of water,
Cool and desirable
I need to taste you
Drain you dry
Feed me this necessity
I'm gasping for, dehydrated, shriveling up into nothing

They all want to fuck me, but they don't want to be with me. I'm worth more than that.

Triple Promise

How can you promise, promise, promise someone
you'll do something and then just not do it?
Without one word.
You never acknowledged it wasn't going to happen.
You didn't apologize when it didn't happen.
I thought I was your best friend.
But it turns out that all you want from me is to take what
I give without giving back.
No more promises.
No more triple promises.
It's time I wash my hands of you.

I Am Amazing

I'm selfless and giving.
I'm stubborn and persistent.
I don't turn my back on people I care about.
I don't throw people under the bus.
I am one of a kind.
Anyone would be lucky to have me as their friend, or their lover.
So why am I so lonely?

Liar, Liar

Your pants are on fire
Lies, lies, lies
I have to tell you pieces of what I know to get you to confess
Then it all spills out
Only when I bring it up
You think I'm clueless
I'm not psychic but I know things without effort
It's a talent and a curse
You then take credit for your confession
I tell you I'm not mad, that your secrets don't bother me
My pants are on fire too
That's the flaw in me
My lack of self respect only hurts me and fuels your lies
Something's got to give
You're a liar and I let you get away with it
That says more about you than it does about me

Too much organization creates much chaos.

Stupid

Stupid, stupid, stupid
I should be in the Corner wearing a dunce cap
It's all just a game for you
You take and take and take
I keep giving in
Dumb, dumb, dumb
My life is a mess
My life feels meaningless
I don't know why I let you in
Every. Single. Time.
I know it's going to explode
I feel stupid because I know
How it ends
And I keep going

Ego

It gets in the way of everything
It makes you blind
It makes you deaf
It makes you lazy, stupid, careless
If your heart was as big as your ego,
I'd be able to break it like you broke mine.

You're wrong. If I knew the heartache you would cause, I wouldn't love you anyway.

Photographs

They're all I have left of your sweet face
A face frozen in time
Forever little, forever innocent
All the smiles and giggles
All the memories of good times and bad,
Happy times and sad
I'm glad to have them but I'd rather trade them
To have you back

Cryptic

Written in sand
Blown away by the wind
Ocean in the morning
Forest at night
Rain flakes and snowdrops fall
I can't make sense of the hidden messages
Quit the games and just
Say what you mean

Hindrance

I'm not used to this feeling,
My head being clear,
Devoid of a medicated fog.
It's hindering my ability to write cohesively.
Was it still me?
Was it a version of me?
A version that can't figure out what's good and what's bad,
Slowing me down?
Or pushing me to be greater?

Sometimes my life feels like a telenovela. It's emotional and impossible to understand if you don't speak the language.

Detox

He's addictive
Like heroin and meth
Coke and cigarettes
A little bit of Captain and
A whole lot of Jack
All the fun stuff that's
Bad for me
The stuff that can kill me
The stuff I crave
I need to go to rehab
Put me under hypnosis
Wipe my memory clean
He's a drug in my body
I relapse every time
I want to be free of this addiction
I need to detox from him
Before he pulls me in yet again

Dating Apps

Men, you can be completely clueless
Sometimes you're assholes
I read your bios
But I don't think you read mine
Men, I'll give you some tips
- Write a bio so we know if we have things in common
- If you don't have pictures of yourself, we swipe left
- In your 40s and still trying to figure it out? We swipe left
- No one cares about the fish you caught
- No one cares about your bare chest
- And, for crying out loud, stop with the gym pictures

I'd rather be single forever if this is the pool I have to choose from

Don't put all your eggs in a basket with a broken handle.

Country Songs

Dolly had it right when she said please don't stop loving me
She had it right when she told Jolene she wouldn't be able to love again
Alana Springsteen has a ghost in her guitar
If I had a guitar, it would be haunted
Brett Young asks for mercy and
So do I
Billy Ray has an achy breaky heart and
So do I
Linda, Reba, Loretta...
They all know how I feel
I won't let it break me
Because I'm going to borrow
Carrie's Louisville Slugger

Fire and Ice

He's hotter than the sun
He's colder than the Antarctic
He wants all the world has to offer
He wants the world to explode into nothingness
He'll make you feel like a diamond
He'll make you feel like coal
He's fire and ice, hot and cold, north and south

Don't worry about the grass on the other side. It's not your grass.

Seventeen

I wish I could go back,
Back in time
Back to when I was 17,
Naïve
Not yet scarred by the evils of the world
Back to the time when I thought love was real
And not just a fairy tale
I wish I could go back,
Back to when I was 17
When some things just didn't matter to a young,
Ignorant girl
I wish I was 17 again

Ugly Peace

It hasn't been easy, and it hasn't been pretty
I always knew I wasn't your only one,
Your safe space
I've always known I was your place holder,
Your constant when others let you down
I was okay with it, until I wasn't
It's not okay and I thought it would hurt more than this
I've made my peace
My hands are clean

They say you always hurt the one you love. But if you love them, why do you hurt them?

Sick

She was never as hurt as she was until she got sick
When the Covid virus ravished her body,
Made her weak
When she had no energy
When she had no one to help her, or a shoulder to cry on, when it was difficult to eat or sleep because of the fever and unrelenting cough
Through sickness and health would never be vowed
She was alone and it hurt all over again

I don't want to work for a living, but I like having food and a roof over my head.

Screw You

I gave everything I had and you took every ounce
And then some
I stayed through it all
I stayed through the tough times, the times I thought would break me, all the red flags
I had hope that it would all be okay
I deluded myself into thinking I was trying to protect my heart when,
In reality,
I was hurting myself more everyday
My loyal heart was your easy prey
You said you were trouble and no one could put up with you and that's the reason for every one of your failed relationships
The truth is that you purposely sabotage every relationship because you don't want them to work
Well, screw you for playing with another's feelings for your own masochist reasons

If you're going to serve it up on a silver platter, be prepared to take a giant bite.

My Sonnet

(Full disclosure: I wrote this as an assignment for one of my college writing classes.)

Rhyming poems is not easy
The whole idea of it
Makes me very queasy,
Makes me just want to quit.
But I will move on
Determined to make it work
Though this work may be frowned upon,
Consider it my own little quirk.
So sit right there
While we muddle through
And try not to compare
To Shakespeare, that is a lot to live up to.
I know my rhymes are a little scary,
So for my grade I say a Hail Mary![1]

---

[1] I got an A. The comment written on my paper was: "Ha! Fair enough."

About the Author

Leah Maye lives in Michigan and has one adult daughter. She's been writing stories and poetry since she learned to write. When she's not writing, she's working her day job as patient service specialist in a physical therapy office. She completed her English Writing studies at University of Colorado Denver. Her other works of poetry include The Best Poetry You'll Ever Read, Whispers, Night: A Book of Poetry, and For What It's Worth. She is the author of Dear Diary, Writing Collections: Stories and Essays from My College Years, The Book of Nonsense, and Instascam: Scamming the Scammers on Instagram.

If you enjoyed reading these poems go check out her other works and leave a review. Thanks for reading!

Printed in Great Britain
by Amazon